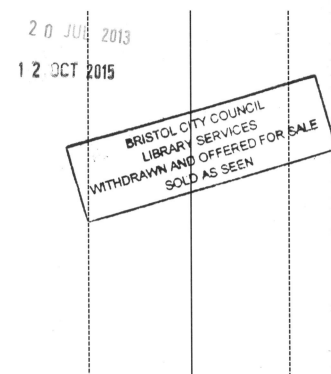

Published by Accent Press Ltd – 2008

ISBN 9781906125936

The Quick Reads project in Wales is a joint venture between Basic Skills Cymru and the Welsh Books Council. Titles are funded through Basic Skills Cymru as part of the National Basic Skills Strategy for Wales on behalf of the Welsh Assembly Government.

Printed and bound in the UK

Cover photo and design by Darryll Corner
Cover photo shot on location at the St David's Hotel & Spa, Cardiff

Quick Reads ™ used under licence

Introduction

Looking back at my schooldays, although I was good at sport and enjoyed playing all sports, I was never the best at anything. While there were always people who were better than me, I had the belief that I could improve and become the best, so I always gave it a go and tried my hardest.

After school, athletics became my life. For years I lived it and breathed it, so when the time came for me to finish competing and make a new life, I was nervous. However, I still believed in myself and my ability to face challenges. It is never easy to try something new but challenges are there to be overcome.

I hope that in this book I can show you how the lessons I learnt in sport inspired and motivated me when I began my new life after athletics.

I started on that new journey at the age of thirty-five. I've proved to myself that you can change direction and learn something new at any time, you really can. It is possible – believe in yourself. You can succeed.

Chapter One

My final race, in March 2003, marked the end of my life as a professional athlete.

After the race, the farewell speeches, the photos and the tears, I felt really disappointed because I hadn't run as well as I thought I should have. This wasn't the way I had planned to leave. I was angry with myself and I remember my coach, Malcolm Arnold, coming over to see me. I said, 'Malcolm, can we find one more race for me to do because I don't want to go out of athletics this way?' Malcolm looked me in the eyes and said, 'When will you ever stop? You'll always find something wrong to make you try again. Trust me, your whole career will not be judged on this one performance today.' I understand now how wise he was.

When I finished athletics, I had to ask myself what I was going to do for the next stage of my life. One part was over, but there was so much more to come. It was very scary, thinking about not being a part of a world I had always known.

I remember a photographer asking to take a picture of me with all the medals I had ever won. He placed them in a semicircle around my head and I didn't actually realise how much I had achieved until I saw them laid out like that. I remember thinking: 'Wow! What a career!' I was European Champion, held Commonwealth Games and three European Indoor titles, two World Outdoor titles, a World Indoor title and had achieved three world records – the only thing I hadn't won was the Olympic Gold!

Then I realised it was all about to stop.

I didn't actually dread getting up the next day but I was a little nervous because everyone was talking about 'The End'. Of course it was really the beginning of a new and exciting time of my life. And above everything else, I was still Colin Jackson from Cardiff – and proud of it. For me, keeping my feet on the ground is very important. Living in Cardiff where I was born and brought up amongst good friends and family means everything to me. My family are very level-headed, down-to-earth people. For them I'm not special, I'm Colin. I think the fact that my parents were always very hard-working set my brother, my sister and me a good example. It's from them that I get the hunger and the desire to try as hard as I possibly can in everything I do. They have also taught me not to crack under pressure and to have a real sense of what's good and what's bad. They set standards. To them, my work was and is no different from anyone else's. The key is to have people around you who are honest and caring. They will always want the best for you.

Chapter Two
Games lessons

My parents, both Jamaican born and bred, came over to Britain in the fifties when hundreds of West Indian families decided to emigrate to Britain – the streets were apparently paved with gold!

They set up home in Cardiff and it was in the Roath area of the city that I was born on 18 February 1967, the baby of the family. I've always hoped that a blue plaque would be put up outside the house to mark the occasion, but to date ... nothing!

I had a very happy and fortunate childhood in that my parents were strict, but, at the same time, very loving. We played lots of traditional card and board games, with snakes and ladders, ludo and Chinese chequers being the family favourites. My mother taught me card games, including a Jamaican version of gin rummy. We didn't play for matches or buttons, just for the win, just for the victory.

My father also taught me at a very early age to concentrate fully on what I was doing. During these games, if he thought for one moment that my mind was wandering, he would invariably come up with some great move and take most of my pieces. There was no fast route to winning – if I didn't concentrate, I'd get beaten, simple as that. Even though these were only games, his words 'Watch what's going on before you make your move' have been a good life lesson for me.

It was the same with table tennis, which we used to play in the garage. My father wouldn't give me a point if he could help it and any loose shot of mine would be smashed back at me. I had to learn the game properly and work at it, and only then could I start taking points from my father and think about winning.

It was he who taught me to concentrate, work hard and be vigilant, and I will always be grateful for that.

When I was four years of age, the family moved from Roath to a new estate in Cardiff at Llanedeyrn. My first school was Springwood Infants and I remember my first headmistress; Mrs George, very well. She was much loved by all her pupils and all around on the classroom walls there were pictures of her drawn by the kids. She, in turn, thought the world of her pupils and spent a lot of time with us and regularly visited our classrooms. Even at the age of four, I was full of energy and used to enjoy sports of all kinds. I remember representing Springwood in a Cardiff and District schools competition and running against five-year-olds ... I came third!

The years passed very quickly and I moved to my secondary school, Llanedeyrn High. It was probably the best in the county for producing winners at the school sports competitions. We had wonderful games' teachers, and many of them had represented Wales in their chosen sports, including rugby, football, netball and diving. I had three gym teachers who were great: Mrs Kenfig, Mr Dyer and Mr Williams.

Mrs Kenfig was special because, even when she shouted at you, you knew why that was. She wanted you to try, to give it a go, to give it your best shot. She never humiliated people, but rather worked on building up confidence and bringing out the best in her pupils and she was prepared to give up a lot of her time to achieve that.

Mr Dyer and Mr Williams were young teachers and real "lads". All the pupils thought they were so cool. They were strict but fair and had a special aura about them. If you were out of line or out of order, they would give you a wallop – worth avoiding. Little wonder that Llanedeyrn High was so successful at sports with such enthusiastic and hard-working teachers.

For me everything was new at this school and I was eager to learn. I loved science; in fact, there weren't many subjects I didn't really like – though geography was one and I wasn't very good at maths or the creative arts. I did enjoy cookery, however (which I still do today), and I can remember cooking breakfasts for my family at weekends. Somehow I managed to stay in the top group for my subjects all through school, something my sister had done some years earlier, and I was proud of that.

In the academic subjects I was like everyone else, just part of the class, but as I got older, I attracted a lot of attention because I was good at sport.

I played basketball, football, rugby, cricket and tennis. I hated the winter sports because they were outside and it was always freezing cold! Every time I was tackled, it was like landing on concrete. The girls were lucky, they were allowed to stay indoors, but for the boys it was outside, and no arguments.

I was a member of the County Championship winning basketball team and played as an all-rounder for the Glamorgan Under 15 cricket team. I was a reluctant outside half at rugby and was drafted into the school football team because I was quick, but I wasn't the fastest runner … even in Llanedeyrn.

I was becoming very keen, though, on athletics and was fortunate enough to represent my county at high jump, hurdles, long jump and even the javelin.

It was really by a gradual process of elimination that I finally came to specialise in the hurdles and it was my coach, Malcolm Arnold (of whom more later), who made that crucial decision.

The 110 metres high hurdles event is very special to me because you have to run as fast as you can and also clear ten three and a half feet barriers in the process. There is a rhythm and a discipline to the event which came fairly naturally, but I enjoyed improving and polishing my performances to be the very best I could.

By now, I had become part of special athletics training groups held in various parts of south Wales and, through it all, my father or mother used to take me in the car to every session. They were always there for me, always supportive, never pushy.

I was sad to leave Llanedeyrn High but athletics was to become my career. Although I was only seventeen years of age, Malcolm told my parents that if I trained really hard I could make the next Olympic team. In Seoul in 1988, four years later at the age of twenty-one, I won the silver medal. Thanks Mum and Dad, thanks Malcolm.

A few years ago when I had retired from athletics, I was invited back to Llanedeyrn to front a healthy eating campaign. I visited my old school and the students asked me what my life was like and what sort of things I did, now that I had given up competitive hurdling. Eventually, someone asked me where I was the night before. I said, 'I was at Buckingham Palace having dinner with Princess Anne.' They were amazed, 'You went to this school and you spent last night having dinner with Princess Anne!'

Sport has brought me some wonderful experiences and I wanted to tell this latest generation of Cardiff schoolchildren that if they put their minds to it, anything and everything was possible.

Chapter Three
Listen and watch

When I announced that I would finish racing, BBC Wales filmed a documentary of my final year. It's hard to watch a whole programme about yourself, but it's a great tribute and I was proud that they wanted to do it. People from my past spoke very kindly about me on the programme and it was amazing to look back at all the places and all the people who have been part of my success. People come and go in your life but memories are very special and I was touched by the genuine warmth of fans and friends from so many places across the world.

The programme included an interview with Malcolm Arnold, my coach, who was such an important influence on me. A coach gives a young athlete life. Malcolm put in a lot of hours, personal hours, to make me the athlete I became. He didn't have to give up all those hours for me. He did it because he was good and had a real pride in what he gave to others. He made time for me and taught me the valuable lesson that investing time in yourself is how to succeed. He was a very fair man and made me realise very quickly that I had to work hard if I wanted to be the best. Nothing comes easy in this game, like in life, and the fact that he taught me that early on helped me as I progressed through my career. He was so solid and I could always rely on him. I valued his honesty – if he thought you weren't doing things well, he was more than happy to tell you! He, more than anyone, showed me how to be proud of my performances. Win, lose or draw, I always gave 100%.

I was committed to the cause, and, for me, the cause was whatever goal was set for that year. Malcolm told the television team that Colin Jackson's 100% is anyone else's 150%. I am proud he thought that of me.

Malcolm's ability to pass on knowledge was the best. He knew how to talk to his athletes. Some people had a problem with Malcolm because he had a very dry sense of humour but I found it very funny. I think we got on well because of that. When I was very young he sometimes threatened to throw me out of the group if I didn't do what he said. Another time, he asked me not to race and I raced. I did it because it was something that I desperately wanted to do. He didn't say why he didn't want me to race, until afterwards. I told him the result and he said, 'When I tell you not to do something, it's for a good reason. The reason I didn't want you to race was because you weren't ready. When you're not ready, you shouldn't try to perform.' As an 18-year-old, I didn't quite understand what he meant, but as I got older I knew exactly what he meant – and he was right!

He taught me to prepare properly for every race. He insisted that I was in the best possible physical shape. If I didn't listen and performed badly, he would always be there to pick me up again. His advice was always good advice.

Once, during training, I told Malcolm that I didn't think circuit training was very good. It would be fine if I wanted to be a world class circuit champion but not if I wanted to be a world class hurdler. He didn't argue but just said, 'Right, if that's what you believe then take it out.' My performances that year were dreadful. He was proved right. Being rebellious doesn't always work, especially when you have a goal in mind and a target to achieve. I learnt to listen to people who know what they're doing. Good coaches, like teachers, are there to help you to reach your heights, so perhaps you should listen to them.

The women in my training group were much better than me and that was quite difficult to deal with. I was stronger physically than the women when it came to circuit training, but they worked harder than I did and that was the reason they were better than I was. A push-up is a push-up whether you're a man, woman or child. A sit-up is a sit-up whoever you are. If you don't work at it, you're not going to improve on it – it's simple. Carmen Smart, Sally Ann Short and Kay Morley-Brown worked harder than I did and they were much better than me in the competitions we held during training. But I learnt my lesson. I understood what was happening and I worked harder to improve things, because I was not going to let it happen too often. And when it came to a race, a proper competition, I always did well. My mind was so strong that I wouldn't let anybody beat me.

I have very much tried to model myself on people who are the best at what they do. When I was growing up, Daley Thompson, the Olympic decathlete, was my hero. People loved his cheeky personality but also recognised his hard work, dedication to the sport and his refusal to give up. He trained hard even on

Christmas Day – that's not a made-up story, that's fact. He always wanted to be better and to have the advantage over his competitors. Daley inspired me. Everyone needs heroes and good examples inspire us all to do better.

Daley's way is to work, but to make work play. He would create a play situation within training to keep everyone going – often some form of competition. I never felt I was training the way he worked because he made it fun and I felt like I was playing ... until I woke up the next day and every muscle in my body was sore. Then I realised I had worked out in a very special way.

Daley had no time for people who made excuses. He once asked me to throw the discus with him and I said my hands were too small. Really, deep down, it was because I couldn't do it very well. He called me to him, put his hand over mine and pointed out there was no difference in size. I learnt so much from things like that.

If you're not good enough that's OK, but don't just say you can't do it. Don't make excuses when you haven't really tried.

Chapter Four
Pick yourself up

Daley Thompson and all the other international sporting stars I have met in my career share a will to win, a passion to succeed. During the filming of the television documentary on my career, I spent time with Jos Andrews, a producer who had the idea that we could work together on an educational project for BBC Wales. She pointed out to me that all the sports people she had met with me talked passionately about the skills they gained from sport. Together, we created *Raise Your Game* for BBC Wales Education and Learning department, an exciting website and television project which includes interviews with a range of sports people from across the world. They share their ways of learning, coping with problems and ideas to improve life skills. Thanks to the support of the Lifelong Learning and Skills department of the Welsh Assembly Government the project became real and schools and colleges are now involved. To athletes it makes complete sense to have training plans, targets and competition dates. It has been a fun project for me but one with a very positive message. By working on this, I have been able to see how much sport can change people's lives. I am very proud to be Welsh and very proud that this is a Welsh project which features the very best from around the world. It's a different way to learn things, a different way to meet new challenges.

The project is aimed at motivating and inspiring people from all walks of life. For me, that's what makes it special. Anybody can use the ideas from the website *www.bbc.co.uk/raiseyourgame* whether it is to find a new job, pass an important exam, lose weight and get fit – the lessons are the same. It's down to hard work.

The website highlights the determination needed by sportsmen and sportswomen to achieve their goals and ambitions through a series of video clips, interviews, diaries and stories. Among those who appear on the site and on the DVDs are Ryan Giggs, Dame Tanni Grey-Thompson, James Cracknell, Dame Kelly Holmes and Haile Gebreselassie. Many of them are good friends of mine. There are five steps to success – Inspiration, Motivation, Preparation, Concentration and Dedication. If you follow these it will help you in whatever you do. I've really enjoyed working with the *Raise Your Game* team to find out what makes other sporting starts tick! So click on and give it a go!

To prove it works, I used ideas from *Raise Your Game* myself when I started learning to ski. I had tried before but took lessons to learn properly after finishing athletics. I saw for myself what it's like to be a beginner in another sport and the least able in the group. I fell down ... and fell down ... It was a painful lesson but I made myself carry on as I didn't want anyone to say I wasn't making an effort. My ski teacher was trying to show me a new style of skiing called carving. It's a very impressive way of skiing and makes beautiful lines with the edges of your skis. It's fantastic when it's done well and the feeling you get is truly amazing. He was trying to show me how to put my feet in the right position and I just couldn't do it. I couldn't quite understand what he was saying and I was feeling more and more irritated about it. Then he gave me a simple idea. I had to transfer my weight from my little toe to my big toe on each foot as I went. That was it – I understood and could see what he was saying. It was a magic moment. I had been having lessons for weeks but nobody had made it clear to me. Sometimes it's just a matter of looking at things another way and for me that really can work. So *Raise Your Game* tries to find different ways of looking at things because there is no one way that works for everyone.

Toes and feet were to play a big part in my life later on in *Strictly Come Dancing* … but that's another chapter.

When you're winning, there's no better feeling on earth. But when things aren't going well, that's the real test. I've often asked good friends in athletics how they cope when things get tough. Everyone has their own way of getting through the bad times but when I spoke to Kelly Holmes, who had suffered so much illness and injury and yet got to be a double Olympic Champion, I found her words a great inspiration.

'I just fight for what I believe in,' she said. 'You've got to have a lot of self-belief and when I think I've been down it makes me more determined than ever to come back.'

I was working alongside Kelly in 1991/1992 and I saw the hardship that she had gone through. In 1996 in the Atlanta Olympic Games, she was so ill, and had so many bad injuries, she virtually hobbled around the track. In the 1500 metres she walked across the line. But she was always so upbeat, even though she was going through so many problems. She still believed she could be a champion. She had a dream and she really believed that she could make it. The Athens Olympic Games in 2004 proved that for Kelly. I was fortunate enough to interview her straight after she had won her two gold medals and I was so pleased for her. She deserved her victories – the way she ran was unbelievable. I was so proud of her; she is inspirational. She won't be beaten and will never give up.

For me, as Kelly suggested, it is about having the drive to keep going even when everything seems to be going against you. It's about working really hard and saying to yourself, 'I can do this.' Don't be frightened of failure and don't use that as an excuse. Go out there and work at it, because people can improve and you have got to have faith in yourself. What is important to me is to put the time and effort in. A lazy soul and a lazy mind create a lazy body.

Sometimes I have put a lot of time and effort to do something and it is criticised. It's easy to start questioning yourself then but the key is to believe in yourself, in what you want to achieve and what you set your heart on. If you give your all, you will achieve success and those people who doubted you will be left behind. Those who doubt you, once you are successful, are always the first to say congratulations. But in your heart, you know that they're not really happy for you. I always say, 'Find out who is there for you when it really counts.'

Back in 1992 at the Olympic Games, everyone was hoping that I'd win the gold medal for Great Britain. I was at the height of my career and firmly believed that I could fulfil a dream and achieve something that is harder to get than an MBE. You don't think of anything else, you don't think of luck, you don't think it's something that you shouldn't get. This is your opportunity to make history and I wanted to achieve the ultimate goal I had set myself. The Olympic Games are what the world judges you by, that is how important the Games are to an athlete. But at the last minute when I was lining up, I knew I was in trouble. I had a slight injury which had happened because I had been quite cocky in the second round. I thought the race was going to be easy and I'd lost my concentration. I had hit a hurdle and it caused me to lose balance and pull a stomach muscle on the left-hand side, and that really finished my chances for the final.

If I had kept my head in the second round and not got injured, I could have won the final. It's easy to look back and say this now but I actually could have done it. What I wanted to achieve on that day in Barcelona was to become the Olympic champion and break the work record in the process. But I took my eye off the target. Instead of just winning the race to become the Olympic champion, I wanted it all. I felt I could win and break the world record because I knew in my heart I was capable of doing that. I wanted it all without seeing what I was doing to myself.

I went into the final feeling really flat and negative. I thought that if I couldn't win the gold medal and break the world record, what point was there in going out on the track? But as an athlete you always think that you can go out there and do something, so when I lined up I remember thinking 'perhaps I can do this'. I pushed out of the blocks and took the first two hurdles and it seemed to be OK. I had a lot of leg speed but my timing and rhythm were out. I ended up making mistakes and hitting hurdles. I remember hitting hurdles four and five and nearly stopping, but something told me to carry on running. Why, I don't know, because there was no way I was going to win the race, but pride was telling me to finish. A lot of people had made a lot of effort and taken time to come to see me do well, and pride was telling me to go out there and give it my best. I started running the other athletes down and I think, going into the tenth hurdle, I was probably second or third in the race. I was moving quickly through the field. If I had just stayed on my feet going into the line, I would have actually had a silver medal. However, I hit the tenth hurdle and virtually fell again for the third time and came in seventh. My time was 13.46, even though I had almost stopped twice after hitting the hurdles. But I lost, and it hurt!

What was so difficult for me was that the winner was my training partner and a good friend. Mark McKoy was someone I trained with every day of my life and he had won the Olympic title, not me. We were, and still are, great mates, but nothing can change the way I felt at that moment. It's a horrible feeling when you know that you are two metres better than someone who has run off with something that you felt should have been yours. It was a tough day for me. I spent a lot of time cheering up people because they were so upset for me. I remember meeting Kay Morley-Brown, a very strong girl and one of my training partners, who was crying as she walked towards me. She was really sobbing and I couldn't understand why she was so upset. I understood why I felt so bad, but why had it affected so many others in this way? Lots of people were genuinely upset that I had lost the race and I felt in some way responsible for that. It's so hard to bounce back from failure because, all of a sudden, you see what you're going to have to live with for the rest of your life. People had really wanted me to do well and I felt I had let them down.

Unlike other big races, there is no second chance in the Olympic Games. If you fail your driving test, you can try it again. If you fail at the Olympics, it's four years until the next one, with no guarantees that you will do better because you may never be in the same physical shape again. That's why it's so heart-wrenching not to get the gold. All that work, all that preparation, all that responsibility and nothing to show for it.

My athletics' life was on a world stage. There wasn't anywhere to hide from what had happened. I heard it on television, on the radio. There wasn't anywhere I could go to escape it. How do you go into your next race coming from that? People have asked me this. 'You came back,' they say. 'What got you into the next race, or who?'

I didn't want to do athletics again. I'm human like everyone else and I did think that my sport had dealt me a bad hand of cards. I felt that I didn't deserve it. I did lose faith in the sport, but of course it wasn't the sport, it was me and the way I had performed on the day that let me down. What the sport had given me was a platform for greatness. And as far as I was concerned, it had also given my best mate my Olympic title, the one that I had worked so hard for ... that was really rubbing salt in the wound.

I was injured, but I was already signed to running events after the Olympic Games. I am honourable and I had to fulfil those commitments. But first of all I had to get my head and body right again. Before I could think of going anywhere I would have to do a time trial. I wasn't sleeping at all because the Olympic nightmare was running around in my brain all the time, and I used to sit in the kitchen just doing nothing when everyone else was in bed asleep. I couldn't shut my eyes.

Every time I did I saw the race again. This went on for four days and on the fifth day I had to do the time trial. I was so tired I didn't know where I was. I didn't want to be there. I warmed up and my muscles seemed fine. I did the time trial out of the blocks, crossed the line and came back to my coach. He said, 'You would have won the Olympic title by over a metre if you had just run like that.' When somebody says something like that which you know is truthful, it just infuriates you even more.

Next, I had to go to Monte Carlo to compete against everyone who was in the Olympic Games yet again and I was dreading the thought of doing it. I remember waiting in the warm-up area before the race and Roger Kingdom, who was the Olympic champion in 1984 and 1988, came up to Mark McKoy who had just won the gold medal and gave him a big hug. 'Hey,' he said, 'welcome to the Olympic club!' I wasn't in that club and I had to accept it, but it hurt. I remember doing my warm-up and they actually kept us apart, the Olympic champions on one side and the rest of us on the other. I didn't feel part of them. I thought: half of my mates are over there and I should be with them. It was awful to be in that position.

I knew I had the ability but my mind was still on that one day when everything had gone wrong for me, and had affected my whole life and career. That's when I realised how important the Olympic Games are to an athlete.

I lined up in Monte Carlo with the Olympic finalists and I pushed out of the blocks. Mark took off, as you would expect of the Olympic champion, but by the fourth hurdle I had caught him. By number five I was running away from the whole field and I crossed the line easily, running a few hundredths of a second faster than when Mark had won the Olympics and I wasn't even trying as hard as I knew I could.

I remember I snatched the flowers from the girl at the finish. I didn't say anything to Mark, I just couldn't. I threw the flowers into the stand to run my lap of honour. As I was running round, I thought to myself: it's just so pointless. I had proved I could be number one in the world. It just hadn't happened to me on the right day at the right time – at the Olympic Games. It was so frustrating and cruel and I struggled to believe it. Every day when I woke up I thought I was dreaming and that it hadn't really happened. Also, I remember thinking:

why can't there be a superman who can just spin me backwards and make me go back in time? If I had another chance, I promise you I would do it right. This time I wouldn't go for a world record if somebody would just give me the opportunity to go out there and do it again. It was so difficult to deal with my failure, but I had to. You can't turn back time.

It took me a long time to make myself forget the shame of the Olympics and think positively. I had to win a global title. I had already proved to everybody I could win races day in and day out, but what I needed was to win a major race – the World Championship. It was a year before that happened. I couldn't wait.

Chapter Five
Champion of the world

The World Championships in Stuttgart in 1993 was payback time for me. I thought I had a real chance of breaking the world record. I was in the best physical shape of my life, and I had just set the European record time of 12.97 seconds – run into a very strong headwind. However, I remembered the big lesson learnt at the Olympics – win the title first and worry about the time later!

The night before the race I wanted to speak to all the family as I knew that they would be going over every hurdle with me. I didn't get to speak to my father – he was too busy washing the car! My sister Suzanne said, 'Tomorrow I'll be putting on my best make-up as I know there'll be cameras outside the house after the race and I want to look my best. You'd better win because this make-up is expensive and I don't want to waste it!' No pressure then!

On the day of the race I did my warm-up not on the major track but on an indoor track where I was out of sight. The other competitors didn't have a clue what I was doing and where. It was just Malcolm and me ... just like a training session! Even the journalists had no idea where the two of us were. Had they known and had they realised we were watching the results come in, it would have been a terrific scoop.

I hadn't been the fastest in the heats but I knew exactly what I wanted to do. The 110m hurdles final was late on in a very long day for me. Before the race, I was alone in a tiny room desperately trying to focus. I wasn't going to fail this time. Outside were Steve Smith and Dalton Grant, the British high jumpers, who had finished their events and were having a noisy game of basketball. It was all over for them. For me, it was about to begin.

Tessa Sanderson and Fatima Whitbread called in to wish me well. Fatima said, 'This is your time to make history and it's up to you.' When she left, I was crying because I was so tense. Then Linford Christie came to check I was alright. He had won his world title two days before. It was OK for him, Olympic gold medallist and now World Champion. Left on my own, the minutes dragged on and on. Why was I putting myself through this? Was it all worth it? The pressure was relentless.

An hour before we were due to leave, Malcolm joined me. I kept delaying getting ready because once you start, there's no going back. Time kept ticking on. We didn't talk. Malcolm sat reading his book while I could only sit. But I couldn't put off getting ready any more. It was time for a shave. Everyone I know has their own routine before going to the track. For me, I had to shave once before the heats and then before a final so that I would look and feel my very best. Then I showered, put some cream on my face and I was ready 'to face the world'. This was my stage and I was ready. If you feel good about yourself, then you'll perform well. I got dressed into my warm-up gear to travel on the bus and also packed my rostrum suit. I was fully prepared, I wasn't going to let this one go.

The bus journey to the track took twenty minutes. Even though it was full of competitors, there was complete silence. Two days before, for the heats, the same group of people had made the same journey laughing and joking. Everyone knew everyone else. At that stage, everyone was confident of qualifying. Today was different. Today was the World Championship final!

The next time I saw the other competitors

was in the call room. I didn't look at them. I didn't talk to them. I wasn't interested in them. This was my time. I prepared my spikes, made sure I had my tape measure and my vest and shorts. This was down to me. Nobody could help me now. I had to pay attention to detail otherwise it could affect the race.

The weather was beautiful, no wind and a packed stadium with 45,000 spectators. When all the finalists came onto the track we faced a long walk to the start line. It was like a parade of contestants in a show. I remember watching Gail Devers, the American athlete, doing a lap of honour, the stars and stripes draped around her shoulders and her lovely smile telling the spectators and the millions at home watching television that she was World Champion. In 1992, at the Olympics, Gail had hit the last hurdle and finished fifth. She had put all that behind her and had now come out on top. I had to go and do the same. Although a lot of people wanted me to succeed, it was only me who could make it happen.

I didn't talk to anyone. I tried to stall the inevitable and took a long time to get to the start. In my practice run, I had hit the first hurdle hard. In the second practice, I did the same. Then I stopped and told myself not to try again. If I'd hit that hurdle for a third time, it would have knocked my confidence. As it was, the others would have seen me hit the hurdles and thought I wasn't on good form ... I'd show them!

A lot of things went through my head. I wanted to prove to those who doubted me that I could win a major race. I wanted my family to be proud of me and I wanted Malcolm Arnold, my coach, to have a World Champion.

When I went down on the blocks, you could have heard a pin drop – absolute silence. Silence, that is, apart from my heart thumping and chest pumping so loudly I felt it would tear through my chest. I got up to the set position, the gun went off and, within two strides, I knew I'd won the race. In the few seconds it took to reach the finish line, I didn't see anybody, I didn't hear anybody, I just let destiny happen. Colin Jackson, World Champion, it felt great. I was ecstatic.

I was front page news on both sides of the Atlantic. I had proved my doubters wrong. I had made it to the top through hard work and a strong will to be the world's best. When the race was over, I threw my vest into the crowd and my shoes went to my sponsor. I kept the medal ... and the memories!

Chapter Six
New jobs, new skills

When I won the World Championship, I also broke the World Record for 110m hurdles with a time of 12.91 seconds. This record lasted for thirteen years. I also managed to break the World Indoor Record. That record of 7.30 seconds for the 60m hurdles still stands.

I had always tried to maintain very high standards and I was proud of my reputation. I wanted my new life after athletics to be just as positive, but what would my new life be?

I had already contacted the BBC and I knew that I had the possibility of working with them as part of the athletics events team and that excited me.

But I did question what I was going to do with the rest of my life. It isn't easy to start again. I was thirty-five and used to being at the top of my game. It's easy to panic because you're not sure where you're going. My life had been very organised. My flights were booked from race to race. My bags were packed and kit planned. I had a list of dates, so I knew where I was going from year to year. That was going to change. I thought about what I wanted to do and how I was going to work to get there. Also, I thought about what I needed to learn in order to do the things I wanted.

I knew I couldn't go into industry or sit behind a desk – not me at all! I needed to discover what I was good at, it takes a lot of time to find out and here I was lucky going to work with the BBC. People there saw something in me that I didn't see myself and were willing to help me. I joined one of the top BBC programmes *Born to Win* as one of the specialists on the series. Sally Gunnell and I were given two teams of youngsters to inspire and motivate. It was a great chance to give back something to the sport I loved … my coach would have been proud of me! I was on network television in a primetime slot and learning a lot. The added bonus was that my new bosses seemed to like what I was doing and so did my new television audience.

Believe it or not, I am really shy. It takes a lot for me to come out of my shell and be relaxed in the company of others. When you are quite good at something, you are happy in your own little comfort zone but the people who really make it are the people who break out of that comfort zone and dare to be different. This was a new world for me and, at first, I didn't have the confidence to feel completely comfortable, but I also knew that this was a challenge I wanted to face and I was determined to do the best I could.

After *Born to Win* came other television opportunities, like *Sport Relief*. This not only taught me about presenting and doing what's called 'pieces to camera' but also introduced me to the world of production. Cathy Barrows, then BBC Talent Manager, told me to take every opportunity to talk to as many people responsible for the final programme as I could. I took the time to talk to cameramen, sound persons, editors and directors – all the creative guys that make a show work.

It sounded very impressive, being in television production. I thought I wouldn't mind doing this. It sounded easy and glamorous with long holidays, short working days and a fantastic social life. I thought, this is for me. Was I mistaken!

I was given lots of information to read and learn about the athletes. I had to know all the facts about their backgrounds, their reports and tests. Research like this is vital in a television programme. You have to know your stuff or you get found out very quickly. I wasn't used to sitting down and reading about people, stuck in an office with no oxygen. I was used to being outside, full of energy, and now they were locking me in a room with an hour and a half to prepare what I was going to say. I thought, I can't do this, I haven't got the skills, and I'm not capable of doing it. At the same time, different people in the office were giving me other work to look through. All this new information was overwhelming. I didn't know what to do. I didn't have the skill to deal with it because I had never used that part of my brain before. What I was great at was hurdling!

I told my boss Dave Gordon, Head of Major Events Sport BBC, that I was finding it hard but I was willing to learn and would put the time and effort in. He simply said, 'Colin, don't take too long learning it.' No pressure there, then! I got the message, the same sort of message that Daley Thompson had given me years before – to just get on with it.

So, learning quickly in a new workplace was another high hurdle for me to get over. In the BBC there is terrific competition to succeed. You are only as good as your last show. I understood that, and that it was a case now of starting from the bottom and working my way up all over again. It was difficult to break through and you can imagine there was a lot of resentment and a little bit of jealousy involved. Like the Olympics, I wasn't a member of the BBC club.

Some people thought I was getting work in television because of my name, not what I had achieved. But I have worked hard to get where I am and I have worked hard to establish my name. So if my name now opens doors, there is nothing wrong with that. That's the way of the world. I'm not going to be embarrassed about it. They wanted Colin Jackson, who had got to the very top of his sport through hard work. Now I had to work even harder to prove to those who had any doubts that I was the man for the job.

I was determined to succeed and set about working for the BBC in the same way as I had done in athletics. Planning and preparing were going to be a big part of my life again. It's funny looking back at my first attempts in front of the camera. They were not great ...

I am far more relaxed now, more natural. I think it's more me and it's a lot of fun.

One of the big problems at the start was

working with talkback in your ear. This is when a presenter wears a special earpiece and through it the director gives instructions about what to do and sometimes what to say. All this happens while the presenter is carrying on with an interview, often live. It's like rubbing your stomach and patting your head at the same time! The very best presenters make it look ridiculously easy and the likes of Claire Balding, Sue Barker and Hazel Irvine, who I've had the pleasure of working with, are just amazing. They deal with the pressure of live television so well and I've learnt a lot just watching them work.

You're supposed to smile, look relaxed, sound intelligent and look as if you know what you're doing. It's tough, and if you don't do your homework and learn the necessary skills, you're out very quickly, because you are easily replaced.

Of course I had been interviewed many, many times during my athletics career but being the man who asked the questions was completely different. At first, I had no idea what to ask people. I didn't know how to get the right answers from them. Looking back at old tapes, I can't believe I was so bad. I wouldn't have given me a job!

I had to improve – and quickly. My next step was to go to media training classes to learn about the job. I saw my teacher as my coach, but the teacher, unlike the coach, had to start from scratch with me.

I was used to being taught but it's different being taught something you are good at and can apply straight away. This wasn't athletics and at first I had no idea what my teachers were talking about. This was a completely new experience with a completely new vocabulary. 'Colin, can you do a PTC, then we'll run VT and in five seconds do an OOV.' I learnt very quickly that this meant: 'Colin, can you do a piece to camera, then we'll run the videotape and you'll talk over that, out of vision.' Wow! It really was hard for me. At times, I thought I wouldn't be able to master it and felt like giving up, but, as with the athletics, I worked and I worked and I worked. Once I had learnt the jargon, I felt part of the group. It's like learning a foreign language. Once you understand it, it makes life much easier and people respect the fact that you've made the effort to learn.

Soon afterwards, my BBC boss Dave Gordon asked me if I wanted to work on the London

Marathon. When you start any new job, you want to impress and you daren't say no to anybody, so I said, 'Yes I'll have a go.' But as soon as those words came out of my mouth, I said to myself, 'You shouldn't be doing this. You're not ready, it just can't happen.'

My job was to talk to the runners about the marathon, why they were doing it and for which charity. It sounds easy but as an athlete I didn't want to stop people in their stride when lots of them just wanted to keep going. It's also very difficult to think of the right questions when you're talking to someone dressed like a banana or a gorilla!

I was really nervous and spent a lot of time worrying about it. This was going to be live television with millions watching ... no pressure again! When the big day came, I was outside Blackfriars, petrified, waiting for my first link. After what seemed like ages, the director's voice said in my earpiece, 'Cue Colin!' My heart nearly stopped. This was it. I was off.

I have no idea what I said or if it made sense. I must have spoken three thousand words in ten seconds because I was so wound up.

It was one of the most difficult things that

I had ever done but I got through it. I was shattered but very happy.

The faith shown in me by my new bosses made me want to improve even more, so I kept up the media lessons. It was like being at school again but this time I wanted to learn! I was taught to write links, prepare notes and speak more slowly. It's no good having a lot of knowledge if you can't get it across. I knew about athletics and I wanted to share my love of the sport with the viewers and listeners. I also learnt about the importance of dress! I've always loved clothes but now I was taught what works on television and what doesn't. Clothes shouldn't distract from what you're trying to say. You can't imagine Gordon Brown giving a speech in a pair of cycling shorts, slippers and T-shirt. People wouldn't take in a word he was saying.

I must have improved, because the next time I was asked to work on the London Marathon I was given a new spot. I moved from a tunnel to a bridge and finally to Tower Bridge, which is the important halfway point. If I hadn't worked hard, Dave Gordon would have left me in the tunnel or locked me in the Tower of London! Instead, he saw potential in me and was happy to go to other departments in the BBC and suggest they give me a go.

Looking back, I am very grateful to those fantastic producers and directors who had such great patience in working with me initially, because they could have been really stroppy. As a young reporter who didn't know his trade, I had to learn my words and do links, which have to be memorised. If you are doing twenty or thirty in a day and you're not used to it, it's quite tiring even if they are short. I was lucky to have producers and directors who gave me a little time to breathe and time to grow and never made me feel inadequate. Often when you are learning new things you become forgetful, you get tired easily and you need to rest. I learnt really quickly that you can't have a late night before doing a piece for the camera because you just won't remember anything. You won't look too good either. It's as simple as that.

As well as formal media training, I decided to do some after-dinner speaking because I thought that would give me more confidence as a presenter and help overcome my natural shyness. My first attempts were terrifying. I had to stand up in front of complete strangers and share with them parts of my life story. Although I wasn't happy with those early speeches, the audience seemed to like them ... but I needed to get better. I took advice from my sister Suzanne who is an actress and she told me to take my time, breathe deeply and be clear in what I said. Now I feel quite confident talking to people publicly. I write all the key points I want to get over on little cards and take time to plan my speech to suit my audience.

I found that the best way to learn was in bite-size bits. Do the research, know your subject, prepare the questions and practise, practise, practise.

I practise learning words all the time, and I am so much better now because I will look at a piece of paper and learn a section of it. What I am doing is training my brain to retain information and then repeat it when I have to. It's not information I need to keep for life, it's stuff that I need to call on when they point the camera at me or when I need to give a speech.

Slowly, people are treating me not as Colin Jackson, the hurdler, but Colin Jackson, reporter and presenter, or Colin Jackson, public speaker, and I'm proud of that.

In turn, I've got to know my stuff and give them what they want, because that's what they pay me to do. Always believe in yourself. If you have done your homework, you should be fine. Initially take one step back, breathe deep, gather yourself and go for it. It's not rocket science.

Chapter Seven
Snow, sharks and sambas

I didn't like dancing. I'm terrified of water and I don't much like the cold. Three of my next big challenges: *Strictly Come Dancing*, *Celebrity Shark Bait* and the Winter Olympics didn't seem obvious career choices.

I had learnt to ski and learnt to ski well; the skill meant I could take holidays with friends from all parts of the world. Like everything I did, I worked hard and was very fortunate to have a good coach again in Bettina, my Swiss friend. I think the Swiss are born on skis. Some years before, I had given Bettina some athletics training and was quite hard on her, telling her to do things like pull-ups and dips. Now it was her turn for revenge! If I was King of the track, she was Queen of the mountains. In skiing you have to concentrate not just on technique but on natural surroundings. It's you, two pieces of plastic strapped to your feet, a pole in either hand and a snowy steep slope. Get it wrong and you're in trouble. Get it right and it's one of the most wonderful, exhilarating experiences.

By now, I was getting more and more work covering summer athletics events, but when the Winter Olympics came around I thought I'd love to be a part of that. I begged Dave Gordon to let me to go. I had found this new passion, skiing, and I wanted to be there. I thought I could ski all day and then do a couple of reports. That was my idea of what it would be like. I was delighted that Steve Cram, another athlete who loves skiing, was also asked to go. (You wouldn't believe that two track athletes who valued their legs so much would take up snow sports and love every minute. But skiing is about style, from your technique to your appearance. A catwalk is not the only place where you can see Chanel, Prada and Gucci.)

I expected a nice skiing holiday in Italy watching some great competitions. The reality was very different. In three weeks I got to ski for three hours, and the rest of the time I was Colin Jackson, the BBC reporter in the mountains. I had to learn about new sports and learn fast. Snowboarding, snowcross, the biathlon, slalom and the super G for men and women, were all new territory for me and luckily I loved it. I had to think and move quickly on my feet. I had to meet new athletes and find out their stories on snow.

Like the Swiss, the Austrians have a great Winter Olympic tradition and, at the time, they were the ones to beat. I was fortunate to have a friend who knew the Austrian ski team very well and, through him, I got some great interviews with them. Michaela Dorfmeister won the women's downhill gold medal. My interview with her in pigeon German had her in stitches, but she was very kind and kept saying, 'Very good'. If only I had made more effort to learn other languages in school!

If working on snow was an exciting experience, diving in water full of sharks was something else, but it had seemed like a good idea when I accepted the job! I was asked if I had a phobia about sharks and I said, 'Not as far as I know … but I hate the water.'

I worked with Richard E Grant. Sometimes he'd phone his best mate who just happened to be Steve Martin, one of my all-time favourite actors! Another of us shark divers was Ruby Wax. I thought: entertain me, that's what you do, and she didn't let me down. There was also Amy Nuttall, an actress from *Emmerdale*. She was fantastic, and so much fun. The whole team got on really well. In the end it was one of the best weeks I've spent in my entire life, but the start was nearly disastrous.

I had to learn how to snorkel and use the equipment, and I nearly drowned during the first lesson. What happened was that I went lower than I should have. All the water flooded into my mask without any warning. I felt this panic attack come over me and it is the only time I have felt really scared in my life because I thought I was going to die. I was deep under water and I knew I was in trouble. If I had let panic take over, it could have seriously been the end. Then I remembered how to handle my nerves. I had been in tough situations before and the way I had got out of them was to keep a cool head.

Those past experiences saved my life and I managed to get back safely to the instructors. What an introduction to scuba diving!

When the time came for us to go down with the sharks, we headed out into this place called the 'shark alley'. We drew straws to see who would go first into the shark cage. Before you go into it, they actually bait the waters so that the sharks will come. When they arrive, they don't arrive alone, but in threes and fours and although they were only about four or five metres long, they looked huge – trust me.

Something the diving instructor said at that time will stay with me forever,

'Ladies and gentlemen, remember when you go into that cage, it will be the first time you will enter the food chain.' When you think about it, he was dead right! Normally you are on top of the food chain, now you could become part of it … it was very scary.

So we drew straws and Ruby went first. She went into the water screaming loudly as they lowered her in. It reminded me of stories about ducking women thought to be witches. Then she seemed to be down there for ever. When she eventually came up she was so excited and said, 'This is superb, it was brilliant, I want to go back down' and I thought: she's having a laugh, she looked terrified before – but no, she really enjoyed it.

Eventually it got to my turn, and I started arguing with the people who were lowering the cage because they told me to sit down in the cage and I was saying, 'How can I possibly sit in the cage because there is nowhere to sit? It's just wire.' However, I learnt quickly to sit down anywhere in the cage because these great white sharks can break out of the water to take their prey off rocks. Anything they can reach, they will go for, and they could knock the cage pretty hard. I was lowered carefully into the sea. The first time you see these ghostly beings, it's amazing. It's very quiet when you are about three metres under water. It's dark, and suddenly they just come at you from the darkness. Then they disappear as quickly as they come. It's terrifying because you know they are just eating machines and wouldn't think twice about taking your leg off. This experience was totally out of my comfort zone – I was out of my depth in every sense. I depended totally on other people to do their job. If they didn't bring me up quickly, hadn't locked the cage properly or put my mask on correctly, I could float out and be eaten or drown. Teamwork was very important and I'm glad I kept all my limbs because I needed them for my next challenge ...

One of the most popular television shows on Saturday night is BBC's *Strictly Come Dancing*. It is family entertainment, combining glitz, glamour, competition and the ever-popular Bruce Forsyth. I had been asked many times to appear in the series but I always had a good reason to say no. I have always shied away from the dance floor, and the thought of making a fool of myself in a shiny costume didn't appeal to me. However, the show's producer kept pestering me and I finally said yes. I forgot about it until twenty days before the recording. The show's researcher rang me up and said, 'Remember you have got to come and meet your dance partner, you have to start training now.' By then, it was too late to pull out. I had committed myself to something, even if I had forgotten about it. There was no turning back now.

I absolutely loved Erin Boag, my dance partner and coach, from the first time we met. She had the right approach for me; she was the right person to teach me. She was really fun but firm, and there is nothing wrong with being fun and firm. We had a great laugh and that is what saw us through. My first lesson was how to move! Running in comfortable track shoes is one thing, dancing in shoes with two and a half inch cuban heels is quite another.

I hated dancing because I felt shy at the thought of people looking at me on the dance floor. I don't mind people looking at me when I can do something properly but the thought of millions watching my attempts to dance wasn't great. When we first met, Erin told me that dancing with me was like riding in a rickety old car, while dancing with her professional dance partner Anton du Beke was like a ride in a Rolls Royce …

However, I knew that if Erin had the patience to allow me to make mistakes I would get there in the end. The confidence that had come from athletics, and the more recent broadcasting, made me realise I could learn and repeat what I had learnt and that nerves weren't going to get to me when I did a live performance. I knew that I could perform in front of millions of people because I had done it before, but could I do it on a dance floor?

Meeting Erin convinced me that I could actually do it. And all the skills I had learnt in athletics could help. I needed to perform under pressure on a new stage. I was a champion, I could win races, and nothing was going to distract me. Once Erin had taught me the steps I would be ready to face the music and dance in front of a live audience. The dance steps weren't mapped out on pieces of paper but worked out on the dance floor by Erin. She would take me to a starting point and say, 'This is your first step, then two, then three,' and so on. We would learn sections of the dance. At this stage, I had no idea how the dance would end, only how it started, but I didn't need to

know the end yet! Learning in bite-size bits ...
I had been here before.

When I prepared for a race like the World
Championships or the Olympic Games I didn't
spend all my time hurdling. It is exactly the
same preparing for a dance competition. You
break everything down into smaller sections.
In athletics, your smaller sections would be
weight training one day, sprinting the next,
hurdling the next and circuit training on
another. You can't do all that on the same day.
It had to be broken down and it was the same
with dancing. You break down the rhythm, you
break down the section of the dance and then
you glue them all together and it should be
seamless.

In this new glamorous world, I was a total
beginner but, again, very keen to learn – the
rumba, quickstep, cha-cha-cha, American
smooth and foxtrot. All these wonderful
dances opened up a whole new world to me. I
didn't stop practising because I had a goal. I
had to dance 'live' on the Saturday. The
programme had a quick turnaround, so I had to
be ready on time. The only sure-fire way of
getting everything done was to work at it. I had
to make the most of precious rehearsal time,
when we had it. Once the rehearsal slot had

gone, it had gone; there was no getting time back. My target was never to go out there and win the show, but to dance the best that I possibly could, and if my best was good enough to stay in, great. I was always happy to stay in and dance for another week.

I never shy away from work, I'm very disciplined. Because I'm not frightened of work, if I'm committed to something I will do it. I'll always put the time and effort in. It was the same for this television series. There are twenty-four hours in a day, so I'd take out the hours I need to sleep and work backwards from there. I don't have to sit in front of television at ten o'clock in the evening. I could actually be learning my dance routine. During the series, I had also been called to be on jury service and I had to fit everything else around that. Dancing is no excuse to dodge jury service!

Dance training changed my life incredibly. It gave me confidence; it took away my shyness and a lot of my inhibitions. It gave me another route to express myself. Although I was a total beginner, I was very anxious to learn well and listened carefully to Erin, my dance partner and coach. That's the way I've always done things.

Dance is all about posture. If you stand up tall and have a sense of pride, you feel better. It's the same with clothes. When you look good in something it gives you confidence. If you feel a million dollars, you act a million dollars.

When I came to the show, people started saying to me, 'You're beautifully lean, you look like a dancer and you're an athlete, so you must be able to dance.' Why? Up until then, I couldn't dance a step. Dancing isn't hurdling. The reason I finally could do it was because I was practising six or seven hours a day in the dance studio. If I started to perform like a dancer, it wasn't because I was a former athlete but because of sheer bloody-mindedness and hard work.

Despite the fact that we had got some good marks and some nice compliments from the judges, we didn't score highly with the tango. I was really upset because it was the only dance I really wanted to learn. But jury service for several days had interrupted our practice. I wasn't ready, I wasn't confident; no wonder the judges weren't pleased. Of all the dances, I thought the tango was nearest to competitive athletics. It has passion, power and great style, that's why I loved doing it. But I wasn't properly prepared and we paid the price.

The other contestants were great. Dennis Taylor in his big glasses gave it his all despite the fact that he knew he wasn't a great dancer. Once a World Champion, always a World Champion. Zoe Ball was always concerned about how tall she was. I thought she was elegant and beautiful! Fiona Phillips and I shared the same dance rehearsal studio and I often had a sneaky look to see how she was getting on ... Always suss out the competition, especially when they're Welsh! I remember the first time we all got together. It was a Friday night, and everyone was excited. We had to do a walk-through so that everyone knew what they were doing and where they needed to be placed. When the music started and everyone began to dance, I thought: wow, this lot are really good!

James Martin, the chef, was dancing with his partner Camilla Dallerup and doing a lot of fancy footwork. I wondered how he'd learnt to do that. Then Bill Turnbull, from BBC Breakfast News, and his partner Karen Hardy did a fantastic cha-cha-cha routine where they kept swapping their hats. It was such an entertaining dance. It was wicked. I really enjoyed it. Then it was our turn. I couldn't tell how we were doing but afterwards everybody said, 'You've danced before.' How little they knew. But I seemed to get away with it! To the crew and the viewers alike, the real competition, however, seemed to be between Darren Gough and myself, as we were both active sportsmen. There was friendly rivalry between us and we had a good laugh together.

I appeared on the programme to learn a new skill, not to win a competition. Although Erin and I didn't win, I made many new friends. And I've got another string to my bow now. At parties, I'm red hot with mums, aunts and grannies!

Chapter Eight
Keep trying, keep learning

I really look forward to Christmas now. In the years when I was a top class athlete, I never once ate Christmas dinner because big races were held in the New Year. I can still remember sitting down to eat tiny portions of food when everybody else was tucking into a turkey dinner. I was a professional athlete at seventeen and I retired at thirty-five. That's a lot of self-discipline and not a lot of turkey!

My new-found freedom has given me new opportunities. There are never enough hours in the day. I'm very hungry to learn and never miss the chance to try new things. I know from my schooldays how difficult it can be, because formal lessons aren't for everybody. It just takes a new way of learning, and sometimes that learning comes later in life. Who would have thought I would have learnt to dance?

I am delighted to be the face of BBC Wales's *Raise Your Game* project. It's a way of learning from the very best sportsmen and women. We all look up to our heroes and can be motivated by their success. Their ideas can be used by people of all ages. The lessons learnt by them in getting to the very top are available to everybody facing challenges.

This project has helped me enormously in preparing for life after athletics. I've taken the practical advice of some of those sports stars I've interviewed and I can tell you, it works! The keys to success are inspiration, motivation, preparation, concentration and dedication. In other words, get yourself ready and go for it!

Over the years, I have learnt a lot about athletics and training for competitive sport. People have often asked me to put something back and do some coaching, and I have wondered whether the things that I had been taught in athletics could be used in other sports. When Mark Foster, a good friend, asked me to help him with swimming training, I jumped at the chance, even though I hate water. Malcolm Arnold, my coach, was a triple jumper, but had taken me on. It was the same for Mark and me. Different sports – but the same goal to improve and be a winner. I wouldn't say I was a fair or a kind coach. I was tough, brutal and intense. I knew what Mark could achieve and I pushed him to succeed. I never once got into the pool or anywhere near the water. I did all my coaching from the side!

But I must have done something right, because he won a World Championship silver medal!

For years I was used to having things done for me. Now I want to start things for myself. I have set up a new company, Red Shoes, named after my winning shoes. It's a small international media company and I look forward to watching it grow and develop.

After years of travelling the world, I realised that while sport is an international language, to actually communicate with fellow competitors and friends needs language skills – which I didn't have. I was fascinated that many of my colleagues on the way to a race could speak one language on a plane, land in another country and be equally comfortable there speaking in another language. I desperately wanted to be the same as them.

The Olympic Games are coming to London in 2012 and I am proud to have been chosen as an ambassador for the event. By then I hope to have learnt Italian and French, and everywhere I go these days I try to take language tapes with me.

When I was fifteen and on my first Welsh Schools athletics course, one of the coaches there told me I would never be any good at hurdles because I was too small. At the time, I was devastated but, very quickly, I was determined to prove him wrong. A few years later Malcolm Arnold, who had spent countless hours helping me achieve my dream, had a World Champion on his hands. Everyone has to start somewhere and if you believe in yourself and are willing to learn from others, everything is possible.

Hurdles are there to get over.

I've had a great life and it's getting better!

Quick Reads
Books in the Quick Reads series

www.quickreads.org.uk

www.quickreads.net

Quick Reads

Happy Families
Adele Parks

Penguin

Lisa is forty-two, divorced and a mum of three. For the past year, she has been going out with Mark, who is five years younger than her. Lisa really likes him but she worries that one day he will leave – just like her ex-husband did. On top of everything else, Lisa feels really tired and moody, and has put on weight. She thinks it's the menopause but could there be another reason for how she's feeling?

Lisa's life is about to change in a big way but does she want Mark by her side? Does he even want to be there? With the help of her family and friends, Lisa starts to believe that a second chance of love and happiness might just be possible . . .

Quick Reads

The 10 Keys to Success
John Bird

Vermillion

Are you struggling to achieve what you want?

John Bird, founder of *The Big Issue*, will show you just how simple success can be.

John gives simple practical tips and advice, such as 'Stop looking for approval from others' and 'Start with small steps'. In this way he shows us that we can all achieve whatever we want. We just need to go after it.

Quick Reads

Doctor Who: Revenge of the Judoon
Terrance Dicks

BBC Books

The TARDIS brings the Doctor and Martha to Balmoral in 1902. Here they meet Captain Harry Carruthers — friend of the new king Edward VII. Together they head for the castle to see the king — only to find that Balmoral Castle has gone, leaving just a hole in the ground. The Doctor realises it is the work of the Judoon — a race of ruthless space police.

While Martha and Carruthers seek answers in London, the Doctor finds himself in what should be the most deserted place on Earth — and he is not alone.

Quick Reads

One Good Turn
Chris Ryan

Arrow

1917, Western Front, Ypres

A soldier wakes up in a damp, dark basement. He can't get out. He is covered in mud. His skin is badly burned. And he can't remember anything. But his nightmare doesn't end there.

He is tried and found guilty of cowardice, impersonating a fellow soldier and theft. He can barely speak, let alone defend himself.

With time slipping away, Chris Ransom must try to remember the events that have led him to this moment, so that he can clear his name and save himself.

Quick Reads

The Hardest Test
Scott Quinnell

Accent Press

Scott Quinnell is one of the best-known names in rugby. He played both rugby league and rugby union, for Wales and for the British Lions. He was captain of the Welsh team seven times and won 52 caps.

But amidst all this success, Scott had a painful secret. He struggled to read. In *The Hardest Test*, he describes his struggle against learning difficulties throughout his childhood and his journey towards becoming one of the best rugby players in Britain. When he retired from rugby in 2005 he continued his battle with dyslexia in order to change both his and his children's lives.

Quick Reads

East End Tales
Gilda O'Neill

Penguin

Gilda O'Neill was born in London's East End. Her nan had a pie and mash shop and her grandfather was a tug-boat skipper. You might think Gilda's childhood was filled with knees-ups in pubs and famous criminals – but that is just half the story. In *East End Tales*, Gilda tells what the true East End was like – not the place of myth and legend. Tales of hardship and upheaval rub shoulders with stories of kindness, pride, courage and humour.

Quick Reads

Humble Pie
Gordon Ramsay

HarperCollins

Everyone thinks they know the real Gordon Ramsay: rude, loud, driven, stubborn. But this is his real story . . .

Gordon tells the extraordinary story of how he became the world's most famous chef: his difficult childhood, his failed first career as a footballer, his TV personality – all the things that have made him the media star that he is today.

Quick Reads

Girl on the Platform
Josephine Cox

HarperCollins

Best mates Mark and Pete board a train to London for their lads' night out.

As Pete finds a seat he notices a girl sitting on a bench. She looks sad and lonely. When the train leaves, he can't get her out of his mind because in her, he has seen a glimpse of himself.

Over the coming months Pete sees the girl often, but when tempted to speak to her, his courage fails. Then one day she simply disappears. Hopelessly besotted by this girl he believes to be his kindred spirit, Pete will not rest until he finds her.

Quick Reads

RaW Voices: True Stories
of Hardship and Hope

Edited by Vanessa Feltz

BBC Books

The BBC's reading and writing campaign (RaW) inspired Vanessa Feltz to compile this uplifting book. In *RaW Voices*, she gathers together men and women who have overcome great difficulties, and asks each to tell their own story. They all show us what we can do to take control of our lives, achieve new goals and reach ever greater heights.

These amazing real-life journeys are a tribute to the strength of the human spirit. Gripping, funny, sometimes sad and always inspiring, they will strike a chord in us all.

Quick Reads

Twenty Tales from Tales from the War Zone
by John Simpson

Pan Books

As a top television journalist, John Simpson has been involved in many dangerous and hair-raising events. *Twenty Tales from the War Zone* brings together the most powerful, shocking and, also, hilarious experiences of his career. It includes amazing stories from the many wars he has covered, from Northern Ireland to Iraq, from Kosovo to Kabul.

Whether crossing the border into Afghanistan disguised as a woman or being kidnapped at gunpoint in the back streets of Belfast, Simpson paints a vivid picture of what being a journalist on the front line is all about. It's a rollercoaster ride that is sure to thrill anyone who dares to join it.

'A first-rate writer and funny with it'
John Humphreys, *Sunday Telegraph*

Quick Reads
Pick up a book today

Quick Reads are bite-sized books by bestselling writers and well-known personalities for people who want a short, fast-paced read. They are designed to be read and enjoyed by avid readers and by people who never had or who have lost the reading habit.

Quick Reads are published alongside and in partnership with BBC RaW.

We would like to thank all our partners in the Quick Reads project for their help and support:

The Department for Innovation, Universities and Skills

NIACE

unionlearn

National Book Tokens

The Vital Link

The Reading Agency

National Literacy Trust

Welsh Assembly Government

Welsh Books Council

Basic Skills Cymru

Communities Scotland

DELNI

NALA

Quick Reads would also like to thank the Department for Innovation, Universities and Skills; Arts Council England and World Book Day for their sponsorship and NIACE (the National Institute for Adult Continuing Education) for their outreach work.

The Quick Reads project in Wales is a joint venture between Basic Skills Cymru and the Welsh Books Council. Titles are funded through Basic Skills Cymru as part of the National Basic Skills Strategy for Wales on behalf of the Welsh Assembly Government.

Quick Reads is a World Book Day initiative.
www.quickreads.org.uk
www.quickreads.net
www.worldbookday.com
www.wbc.org.uk/worldbookday
www.gwales.com

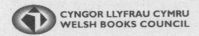

CYNGOR LLYFRAU CYMRU
WELSH BOOKS COUNCIL

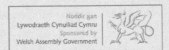

Noddir gan
Lywodraeth Cynulliad Cymru
Sponsored by
Welsh Assembly Government

Words Talk-Numbers Count
Geiriau'n Galw-Rhifau'n Cyfri

Other Resources

Free courses are available for anyone who wants to develop their skills. You can attend the courses in your local area. If you'd like to find out more, phone 0800 66 0800.

 Don't get by get on 0800 66 0800

A list of books for new readers can be found on www.firstchoicebooks.org.uk or at your local library.

The Vital Link

Publishers Sandstone Press (www.sandstonepress.com), New Island (www.newisland.ie) and Barrington Stoke (www.barringtonstoke.co.uk) also provide books for new readers.

The BBC runs a reading and writing campaign. See www.bbc.co.uk/raw.

 In association with RaW

2008 is a National Year of Reading. To find out more, search online, see www.dius.gov.uk or visit your local library. In Wales, the National Year of Reading is supported by the Welsh Assembly Government and coordinated by the Welsh Books Council.

www.quickreads.org.uk
www.quickreads.net
www.worldbookday.com
www.wbc.org.uk/worldbookday
www.gwales.com